Getting to Know
Greece

ILLUSTRATED BY *Don Lambo*

Getting to know
GREECE

Regina Tor

FREDERICK MULLER LIMITED   LONDON

Author and publisher wish to acknowledge with appreciation the courtesy and technical assistance given by the Greek Embassy in New York, through Mr. John A. Tzounis, its able Director, who checked the manuscript of this book for accuracy of fact and interpretation and made invaluable suggestions.

Printed in Great Britain by Jarrold & Sons Ltd, Norwich

With love for Mother and Dad Shekerjian

JUTTING DOWN FROM Europe into the Mediterranean Sea, Greece looks a bit like a bony arm with a four-fingered hand—a shape cut with such jagged edges you wonder if maybe it was meant to be a piece in an intricate jigsaw puzzle.

The arm separates the Ionian Sea on the west from the Aegean Sea on the east. The hand, called the Peloponnesus, points its short green fingers into the Mediterranean.

Except for its northern border, which it shares with Albania, Yugoslavia and Bulgaria, and for its north-eastern border, which it shares with Turkey, Greece is surrounded by the sea—three seas, all emerald-blue and dotted with hundreds of islands which glisten like jewels in the sparkling sun. These islands, as well as the mainland, are Greece.

On the south-eastern edge of the mainland, just across the Corinthian Canal from the Peloponnesus, lies the city of Athens, the capital of Greece.

7

Athens is a large city of one million people—a modern city with tall buildings, rushing taxis, crowded buses, smart shops and department stores, gay cafés; a city of honking horns and blinking traffic lights—a great centre of trade, industry and finance.

Yet, at the same time, Athens in many ways is still a Greek village. Down the modern streets, past the modern stores, come the farmers from the country, the fishermen in from the sea. They merge and blur with the smartly dressed crowds, become a part of the city which is Athens.

Summer comes to Athens and to all Greece about the middle of May. The sun grows orange-warm, bees hum, frogs croak in the heat—dust thickens in the streets. In Athens the people get up early, while it is still cool. They breakfast lightly, then work until lunchtime. After lunch, shops and businesses close their doors and the people rest behind closed shutters until 4 o'clock in the afternoon.

It is too hot to work. It is so hot that policemen stand under striped umbrellas. The air is so dry and dusty, little boys wait at restaurant doors with feather brushes to flick the shoes of those who come to eat.

Summer evenings in Athens are gay. The cafés put their tables out on the pavement and everywhere people sit enjoying ices, cups of Turkish coffee, glasses of wine. The air hums with people talking, laughing—the call of boys selling flowers or pistachios from baskets—with the distant shouts of children at play. As

the people talk and sip, dusk deepens in the streets. Nightingales warble in the Royal Garden. The hawkers leave the square, taking their pushcarts of pins, perfumes, ties and sweets, and turn up the streets to home. Night breezes stir. The air cools, and people begin to think of food. In summer everyone eats in the open air, but rarely before 8 or 9 o'clock.

It is fun to eat in Athens. In many of the *tavernas*, or restaurants, you go into the kitchen, look into each of the huge steaming copper pans, sniff, and make your choice—lamb with beans, veal, fish, pilaff, or perhaps kokoretsi? Kokoretsi is little pieces of liver, heart and kidneys wrapped tightly in lamb's intestines, strung on skewers and broiled over charcoal. Delicious!

Athens is busy in the summer-time. Every year visitors come by the hundreds to this city where long ago lived a people who changed man's thinking for all time to come—a people who gave to the world the basis for a democratic civilization. The tourists come to see the ruins, to visit the remains of buildings in which these ancient people lived and worked and worshipped their gods.

Perhaps the most visited ruin is the Parthenon. It was built almost 500 years before Christ was born, as a shrine for the goddess Athena, goddess of wisdom and patron goddess of Athens. The Parthenon is so beautiful it has inspired architects of every age in many countries.

To reach the Parthenon you must climb the steep steps up the rocky hill called the Acropolis. Yellow mustard and cactus grow among the rocks, and children fly bright red and white kites on the summit. The strong, towering, yet delicate-looking columns of the Parthenon change colour as the day progresses. At dawn they are pink, then amber and warm orange at mid-day. As the afternoon grows older, the colours change to violet, mauve with streaks of turquoise blue. Finally the columns become white in the moonlight. Only in the moonlight do they look white, for over many hundreds of years the sun has tanned the marble, and standing as they do high upon the hill, the columns catch and hold each colour of the day.

Like the Parthenon, each temple in Greece was built for a specific god or goddess. There were temples built for Zeus, father of gods and men, for Venus, goddess of love and beauty, for Apollo, the sun god, for Hermes, fleet-footed messenger of Zeus, and for many, many more.

Mythology is the collection of stories about ancient gods and goddesses and heroes. Most of the myths were explanations of things in nature—how men, animals, trees, flowers, the sun, the moon and the stars came to be. For example, the myths explain that thunder and lightning are caused when Zeus hurls his thunderbolt. A volcano erupts because a terrible creature is imprisoned in the mountain and every now and then struggles to get free.

Some myths, of course, explain nothing. They are just amusing stories about the gods—the sort of thing people might tell to each other on a long winter's evening.

The gods and goddesses of Greek mythology were human gods. They looked and acted like men and women, and the Greeks, although they feared the gods' anger, felt at ease with them, felt free even to laugh at them. And always they built beautiful temples for them.

The Parthenon is just one of many ruins in Athens. Archaeological groups from many countries are forever digging and forever finding new remains of Athens' ancient glories. Some have been completely restored. On one of the temples, the Temple of Zeus, is inscribed:

> *This house was built for Zeus, where he will find*
> *In Athens the Heaven he has left behind.*

This, perhaps, best describes how the Greeks still feel about their beloved city.

Athens is exciting and Athens is beautiful, but Athens is just one small part of Greece. No matter where you go in Greece, it is beautiful—the sky that seems to be always blue, the brown bones of mountains rising up around the soft green fields, the cliffs that slant straight down into the sea, the haze on the hills, the heady smell of wild thyme and lemon, and everywhere the sun, the bright, bright sun.

Yes, Greece is beautiful. But Greece is also poor in the one thing that every country needs—good farm land. Greece has so little good soil, she tells this story about herself:

"When the world was made, God put all the earth through a sieve. He set some good soil down here, and this was one country. And He set some down there, and that was another country. And so He went on, and when He was finished, He threw all the stones over His shoulder, and that was Greece."

It is a good story, for more than two-thirds of Greece is mountains, stony, rocky mountains, many barren of anything except scrub for thousands of nimble-footed goats. Yet, in spite of the mountains, most of the people work on the land. The farmer, always in great need of more land, farms even the lower slopes of the mountains. He has terraced these with stone walls to keep what soil there is from washing away. From these tiny fields he takes a small harvest for himself.

Towards the coast and in the folds of the mountains are the plains, some of which are very fertile. More than one half of the people live on these plains and coastal stretches. In these areas the farmer has a slightly easier time, but even here he must work from dawn until daylight fades from the sky to get enough from his narrow fields to feed his large family.

Surrounding the plains are the wild, empty mountain landscapes, heather- and pine-covered. As the roads twist and climb between the rocks, the air grows thinner and colder. The only life one sees here is the lonely shepherd in his shaggy goatskin coat, watching his flocks as he must have done in Biblical times.

Greece, although only slightly larger than England, has two climates—a temperate climate in the mountains and in the river valleys of Thrace and inland Macedonia, and a Mediterranean climate on the coasts and in the islands. Where there is a Mediterranean climate, winters are usually short and mild with warm rains to water the land. Where there is a temperate climate, the winds blow down from the north, and snow piles soft and deep in the mountain passes, hangs heavy on the pines.

When the snow begins to fall in Greece, the shepherds come down out of the hills, driving their flocks before them. They spend the winter in their village homes, sipping coffee in the coffee-houses, talking and carving, maybe, a new crook or a drinking bowl from a chunk of wood.

21

The shepherd of Greece leads a solitary nomad life. Early in the spring he takes his hardy sheep and wayward, nimble goats up to the high mountain reaches. There, scattered over the terrifying slopes, the flocks crop the thin herbs. A goat, as you know, is a bit of a show-off. He takes a stance on a craggy height, pauses, silhouetted against the sky, and then leaps. From rock to rock he leaps gracefully, gaily, and his bell tinkles with a sound like running water. But the goat, although seemingly gay, has a responsible position in Greek life. The majority of people depend on him for both milk and cheese, and to the shepherd he gives his skin for a coat.

The shepherd is a tough, self-reliant man, whether he is old or young. For weeks on end he lives alone on the mountainside, watching his flock, playing his reed pipe, with only his shaggy shepherd dog for company. When night comes, he lights his lonely fire and gathers his flock into a fold built of branches.

Most shepherds still wear a hooded coat and the *fustanella*. The fustanella is a white shirt with very wide, uncuffed sleeves, over which is worn a blue or white wool waistcoat with black braid and sometimes silver embroidery, and a short, very full, pleated white skirt. This skirt is made of about 40 yards of material. A sash is worn around the waist, and the costume is completed with the addition of long white stockings, red shoes with pompons, and a red cap with a long black tassel. The fustanella is the national

Greek costume, but it is worn today only by men in the mountain regions and by the Palace Guard in Athens.

PALACE GUARD

Approximately three-quarters of the people in Greece live in villages and are dependent upon farming for a living. The average farm is small, often not more than three or four acres. Often these acres consist of narrow fields located in various parts of the countryside surrounding the village in which the farmer lives. The farmer, whose fields are located far apart, spends a good part of his day walking from one field to another.

The donkey is the beast of burden in all Greece. Never complaining, always patient, the donkey works from dawn to dusk balancing two huge, heavily laden baskets, one on each side of his bony body.

There are all kinds of donkeys in Greece. There are the vegetable-donkey, the fruit-donkey, the flower-donkey. The flower-donkey, of course, is the most loved, for his flowers are bought for love—red tulips, purple, pink and red anemones, roses, violets, yellow pansies, blue irises, and the beautiful white almond blossoms.

The vegetable-donkey, with his owner, appears in village streets in the morning:

"Marrows to sell! Marrows, aubergines, potatoes, tomatoes! Tomatoes! I have sweeeeeeet tomatoes!"

The chant breaks the stillness of the summer dawn, wakes the cooks and the housewives. Doors open, and the day begins. The cook asks the price. The hawker answers—not simply, you understand, but sailing off in lengthy poetic praise of his beautiful vegetables. Finally, after a great deal of agreeable argument, a price is decided upon, the purchase is made, and the hawker and his donkey go on to the next call.

They do not have far to go because Greeks do not like to live alone, apart from their neighbours. You never see a lonely farmhouse in Greece. Greeks build their homes close to one another in the villages. They like the companionship of a cup of coffee shared, the comfort of talk and troubles aired, the pleasure of planning together for the festivals of Easter and Christmas and St. Basil's Day.

Greeks love to talk—to argue about politics, debate world affairs, discuss the nation's problems. To be able to speak well is an art, and almost all Greek people are persuasive and keen-witted in their talk. Many have the unusual ability to be both poetic and logical at the same time. In the villages particularly, many of which are isolated from each other by the mountains, talk is one of the few diversions available and is a much-practised art.

The average village is small, with from one to four hundred houses and between five hundred and one thousand people. In a typical village, whitewashed stone-walled cottages line the streets

where people, sheep, goats, shaggy shepherd dogs, donkey-drawn carts and a few chickens all walk. Once in a while a lorry lurches by, or a bus draws up scattering a cloud of dust. Children play in the sun, in the shadows of trees—a game of tag, a game of "statues", their shouts of laughter ringing in the clear blue day. Now and then a donkey brays. In the middle of the main street stands a stone water trough, fed by a well or a spring. Here the women and girls come with pitchers and pails to draw the family's water supply, to wash the family's clothes, to chatter and talk, exchanging the latest titbits of gossip.

The average village house has three or four rooms, floors of hard earth or soft wood, whitewashed walls, and shutters at the windows to keep out the sun. The few chairs are straight and hard. There is a table and low, unadorned beds which are almost as hard as the chairs. Family photos and holy pictures hang on the walls. A small stove in the combination living-and-bedroom is used mostly for cooking. Because fuel is scarce and expensive, the stove is used for heat only when the winter turns very cold. In villages where there are no electric lights, small kerosene lamps are lit after sundown. Electricity is now being supplied, however, to many villages and, under the electrification programme, it will one day be carried to the most remote corners of the country.

On long winter nights, while the mother weaves or mends the clothes, the father tells a story and the children, listening, make black shadows against the white walls. There is the good smell of bread baking, a soup stewing. The house grows steamy-warm, content, secure against the cold winds outside.

Villages clustered in the sheltered angles of the plains, or sitting astride the roads which twist around the hills and across the plains—villages on the seashore—villages in the mountains, and villages too high in the mountains to be lived in when winter comes—in all these, life goes on much the same as it has for hundreds of years.

Everyone in the family works hard, even the children, who at a very early age share in the tasks of daily living. Greek children work in the fields if their fathers are farmers—by the seashore or aboard a boat if their fathers are fishermen or seamen. In the mountain areas children help to graze the herds of sheep and goats.

The Greek child spends most of his time out of doors learning how to work, and also how to make his own toys of pine cones and sea shells. He makes flutes from bamboo or from birds' bones. If he lives by the sea, he makes his own fishing rod and tackle. Young girls learn to help their mothers at home. They learn to spin, weave, embroider, and to care for the smallest children in the family.

In Greece the mother often joins the father in the fields. While her baby sleeps in a cradle under a tree, she bends over the hoe or sickles the wheat. At night she returns home to cook, clean, wash, sew, mend and sometimes weave the cloth for her family's clothes.

Many evenings after work and on Sundays, while the women do the household chores, the men go to the coffee-house to sit and talk, to laugh, discuss their crops, or perhaps to play a game of draughts or backgammon. They share the newspapers and argue over the news. When they can afford it, they have a small cup or two of thick Turkish coffee or a glass of wine made from local grapes.

In some villages there might be one or two "rich" farmers who own maybe 80 acres of land each. Their homes are more comfortable, with six or seven rooms, beds with bright woollen blankets and factory-made cotton sheets, more tables and chairs, and perhaps a gramophone.

In the village, the people grow much of what they need. Their fields of wheat give them their black home-baked bread. Their groves give them olives and olive oil. From their flocks they get goat's milk and goat's-milk cheese (salty and sharp) and sheep's wool to make into clothes and coverlets. Fruit, eggs, beans and other vegetables, meat maybe once a week, and fish for people near the sea complete the diet. For the richer farmer, meals are basically the same—more fruit, more vegetables and more meat being the only difference.

The church is always the finest building in any Greek village or town. It is usually of stone, this being the most available material, and often quite imposing. In all Greece there is no sound more characteristic of the country than the sound of church bells ringing —marking the holy hours and the holy days, days of feasting and

GREEK
ORTHODOX PRIEST

days of mourning. They can be heard even out at sea.

One of the most distinctive sights in Greece is the priests with their long beards, their tall black hats, and their full-flowing black robes. In many villages the priest is as poor as his people and must work in the fields as the others do to support his family. Most of the people are Greek Orthodox, and their lives revolve around the calendar of the Church.

Entertainment in the village consists mostly of families visiting and families celebrating the feast days of the Church. There are no cinemas, as there are in the cities, but there are many feast days and holidays and at these times the people join in singing and folk-dancing in the village open spaces. For these, the women and girls wear historic costumes

31

—brightly coloured, full-skirted costumes with beautifully embroidered aprons and strings of gay, bright beads or coins of gold. The carnival season before Lent, and Easter week at the close of Lent, are the best times of all for feasting and holiday-making.

At Easter every family has its roast lamb—the Paschal lamb. On Good Friday the ceremonial bier is carried in procession through the streets and the fields, before the priest receives the holy icon again into the church. An icon is either a wooden plaque or a piece of tapestry on which is painted or woven an image of a saint, or a group of saints, or Christ. The icon used at Easter shows the figure of Christ. The icon rests in the bier, which represents the tomb of Christ, and the bier is decorated with white carnations and white lilies and is lit with white candles. It is very impressive.

At midnight on Easter Saturday, the people break their Lenten fast. After the chanting and the long wait in church, while everyone holds a lighted candle and little children wriggle with impatience, the hour comes at last. *"Christos anesti!"*—"Christ is risen!"—"Truly He is risen!" Then everyone goes home and eats lamb roasted on a spit over charcoal. The breakfast eggs, the Easter eggs, are hard-boiled and dyed red.

The people of Greece celebrate with joy the great feasts of the Church—Easter, Christmas, and the various saints' days. There are many saints to celebrate and small wayside shrines are found along many of the roads in Greece. More of these perhaps are dedicated to St. Nicholas than to any other saint. St. Nicholas is the patron saint of Greece, the same St. Nicholas who made his way around the western world and finally arrived in Britain as Santa Claus.

In the villages, traditional folk dances are always an important part of the holiday celebrations. In most of the dances, the dancers stand in a semicircle, holding hands or holding the ends of a knotted handkerchief. Only the leader performs. If the leader is a man, he leaps and twists. If the leader is a woman, she steps and turns primly. The other dancers move together, swinging with the lilting music. The songs they sing have been handed down through hundreds of years and are usually accompanied by a violin, a clarinet, and sometimes a *lauto*, which is similar to a lute.

Christmas is also a time for great celebration in Greece. The holiday begins on the morning of Christmas Eve with the coming of the Kallikantzari. The Kallikantzari are mischievous goblins who come popping down the chimney at Christmas-time and immediately get into all kinds of trouble. They put out the fires on the hearth, they spoil the cakes and the biscuits, they throw mud into the food, the milk and the water. They tangle up the horses' tails and blow out the lanterns. They ring church bells, turn the pages of the priest's Bible, break the thread of the spinner and the weaver. They trip people up, whistle in their ears, spill their coffee, burn their bread. To say the least, they are exasperating pests.

On the 6th day of January, however, their fun comes to an abrupt end. On this day, the Day of Epiphany, the priest throws the cross into the water. Then the Kallikantzari rush pell-mell back to their haunts. To make sure, though, that none lurk behind, the priest goes from house to house, sprinkling holy water everywhere to bless the home.

On Christmas Eve, before the family goes to Mass, young boys gather in groups and go carolling. Their singing is accompanied by the beating of small drums and the tinkling of steel triangles. In some parts of Greece, the boys make torches by tying empty cans to long sticks and filling the cans with turpentine collected from pine trees. The turpentine, when lit, makes a beautiful torch.

For Christmas, children receive figs, walnuts, almonds, cakes and sweets. When parents can afford it, children also receive money. There are no presents for Christmas, and no Christmas tree. Christmas is basically a religious holiday and a family feast. In Greece, children receive gifts on St. Basil's Day, the first day of the new year.

After a twelve-day holiday for Christmas, children all over Greece return to school. The village school is often not as impressive as the church, for so many of the schools were destroyed in the last war that it was necessary to repair them in a hurry. These schools are usually made of stone or brick and often they have no more than three or four rooms. They are usually very crowded. Many new schools, however, have been built and these are modern buildings with big windows and airy rooms. In all primary schools, both new and old, learning is mostly done by memorizing and reciting.

In the towns and cities there are large primary schools very like English ones, and grammar schools and, in some towns, agricultural and commercial schools. Primary and grammar school both

have 6-year courses. The school year begins in September and ends in July. A Greek child enters school when he is six and goes to school six days a week.

In primary schools, children learn reading, writing and arithmetic; geography, history, science and citizenship. Special emphasis is placed on the teaching of religion, and music, art and physical education are included in the list of required subjects.

Grammar school education is not free and is not compulsory. It is divided into two types—the *"practicon lykeion"*, which stresses science, and the *"gymnasion"*, which stresses classical studies. After grammar school the student may enter one of the universities.

Many of the words we use every day come directly from the Greek language. Did you know that the word "arithmetic" is Greek?

The word "arithmetic" actually means "having to do with numbers", as you have probably guessed. Geometry, too, had its beginning among the ancient Greeks, and English grammar school students today still pore over geometry problems laid out by the Greek mathematician Thales, 600 years before Christ was born. In fact, all our present-day physical science has its basis in the system of exact and orderly reasoning developed by the ancient Greek mathematicians.

In many other fields, too, the influence of the ancient Greeks is still very easily seen. The technical vocabulary of medicine is Greek and all doctors still take the "Oath of Hippocrates". Hippocrates, the Father of Medicine, lived and taught in Athens about 400 years before the birth of Christ.

Our cities are full of buildings copied from Greek temples, and statues of the ancient gods and goddesses decorate many of our parks and public buildings. Hermes with the winged feet appears on the windows of florists who advertise flowers by wire. Pegasus, the winged horse, is the emblem of the Parachute Corps. Atlas can be found on the cover of many geography books. The name Venus appears on a well-known pencil, and, if you look around, I'm sure you will notice many other familiar objects with Greek names.

The Greek words *"Kyrie, eleison!"* (Lord, have mercy upon us) occur in the solemn sacrifice of the Mass in every Roman Catholic Church in Britain every day of the year. The same words are also used in English in the services of the Church of England.

Our word "gymnasium" comes from the Greek *"gymnasion"*— the house where Greeks practised their athletics and, in ancient times, where the young men were taught. The word "athlete" too is Greek. It means one who contends for a prize.

Everyone has heard of the Olympic Games. The beginnings of

these are lost in antiquity but tradition associates Hercules with them. The first recorded date for the games at Olympia is 776 B.C. At that time they had great religious significance, and were closely tied in with worship of the gods. There were chariot races, boxing, wrestling, running races, discus throwing, and throwing the javelin. The games were held every fourth year until A.D. 394, when the Roman emperor Theodosius I forbade the worship of old gods and closed all the temples.

GREEK CHARIOT

Fifteen hundred years later, in 1896, the games were revived as an international event. After this date they were held every four years, except for the war years, each time in a different country. Modern Olympics have no chariot races, but to the ancient games we have added tennis, swimming, fencing, ski-ing and other modern sports. Young people from almost every country in the world today work hard to win the Olympics.

The Greek town differs from the village in many ways. The average town has electric light, a cinema, many small shops, several restaurants and coffee-houses, and sometimes a hall for dancing. There is often a hotel for tourists, and some of the streets are paved. The square, or *platea*, is a big open space near the centre of the town and is bordered by the principal stores and cafés and the most important church. In the evening the young people promenade on the square—the boys and the girls in separate groups. On holidays they form great milling throngs.

In the town, the houses of the community leaders, the merchants and the lawyers, are usually two-storied and sometimes spacious. In the town there is a mayor—in the village, a president—who keeps the records and generally governs the affairs of the people.

Many of the towns are charming, with streets shadowed by white poplars or tall cypresses, chestnut, beech and oak trees. Shops are bright with bales of plain and patterned cottons for dresses. Golden oranges and wild lemons are arranged in orderly piles between the figs and the grapes, the baskets of pale eggs. Fresh joints of meat hang on pegs on the walls of the meat shop. Next door stand neat stacks of baskets, pots and pans, new earthen water jars. There is a bustle in the streets, women shopping, women talking, and a lively interest in everyone's business.

A bus loading up for Athens stands in the square, baskets of produce roped on the back. People jostle each other clambering aboard—women with chickens tied together in bunches, men with all kinds of fruit and vegetables and fragrant flowers, children, tired and tugging at the various skirts and trousers legs. People call to one another. Noise fills the street. Everyone, it seems, is going to market.

In the evening, in the restaurants and cafés, men gather to talk—gossiping, arguing, incessantly discussing. The women can be found at home working, or fetching water from the spring, or sitting on their doorsteps resting, and gossiping too, while their children play in the gathering dusk.

Almost every town and village in Greece had its beginning in antiquity. In many, broken columns and massive stone monuments, relics of a remote past, stand side by side with modern buildings and intricate machinery. All over modern Greece, ancient Greece exists as a background against which the life of the country flows on.

In autumn and in spring, the earth is sown. In May the corn in the lowlands is already yellow, and men and women, boys and girls are all reaping the harvest. In many places the farmer still threshes his grain on a circular stone threshing floor beside the field. He strews the sheaves thickly over the floor, and then over this he drives his mules, round and round and round. Sometimes a woman takes over this job, and then her child rides too, standing between the mother's ankles and gripping her bare legs—laughing, delighted, round and round.

Although in some areas today tractors and other machines are being used, many Greek farmers still use primitive tools. This is especially true in those places where the fields are hilly or rough with stones. Many farmers still push small, home-made ploughs behind skinny mules or oxen. They sickle the wheat and winnow it in the wind. They hack at the dry tough earth with hand-made

hoes. And the earth of Greece is very dry and very hard, for the summers are long and hot and practically rainless.

In some areas farmers' co-operatives have helped to install irrigation systems (as the government has also done), and in some communities co-operatives help the farmer with loans of machinery, the distribution of fertilizers, and aid in the marketing of the harvest. In recent years these co-operatives have grown to large numbers. With their assistance the life of the Greek farmer is steadily improving.

When autumn comes the harvest begins, and all over Greece people work late in the fields. One of the important harvests is that of the currants which are grown around the city of Corinth. Currants are actually tiny seedless grapes which are sun-dried, a special kind of grape that for many years would grow only in Greece. The currant harvest is exported almost entirely to England, where currants are used in many kinds of cakes, puddings and bread. Doesn't your mother put currants in her Christmas fruit cake?

The olive harvest is also very important. Olives are a leading export. Also Greeks eat olives with their bread, and olive-oil is an important ingredient in every dish.

From October to December men, women and children, each with a long stick and a basket, work in the olive groves. When the olives are ripe, the harvesters beat at the trees with their sticks, and down fall showers of fruit. From dawn to dusk the groves echo with shouts and songs and laughter while the leaves flutter with the beatings and the earth turns green-black with the fallen fruit. Greece exports not only whole olives, but is also one of the principal olive-oil-producing countries of Europe.

Figs, oranges, tangerines and lemons are also exported. The next time your mother brings home a packet of figs, see if the label says "Kalamata" figs. Kalamata is a green valley on the southern tip of the Peloponnesus, terraced as evenly as stairs and closely planted with lovely fig trees, pink-flowering almonds, and rows and rows of silvery-green olives. Kalamata, like many Greek towns, looks warm and creamy with its mellowed white stucco walls and faded red tile roofs.

The Peloponnesus is a delightful mixture of fields golden with wheat and fields green with vineyards and ripening corn, gnarled olive trees and pine-clad valleys—a mixture of rugged beautiful mountains, peaceful fields, ancient ruins and modern towns. From Patras, the third largest seaport in Greece, is shipped the bountiful harvest of the land.

Tobacco is the most important export. Grown mostly in Macedonia and Thrace, this tobacco is called "Turkish" because these two northern provinces, which have always grown tobacco, were once part of Turkey. Turkish tobacco is an ingredient of many English cigarettes.

Thrace is actually no more than a narrow strip of land which

TOBACCO LEAF

stretches along the coast of the Aegean Sea between the mountains and the sea, but its moist river deltas are ideal for the growing of tobacco.

Macedonia is a much larger province. In addition to tobacco, Macedonia has grass and cattle on its plains, wheat, beans, corn and cotton.

Wheat has always been grown in Greece, but wheat until very recently was one of the Greeks' most important imports. Today, thanks to improved methods of cultivation and better seed, Greece produces all the wheat she needs for her bread. Dairy products continue to be imported, however, because summers are too hot and dry to grow the grasses cows need and also because, even if the summers were cool, there isn't enough land to spare for grass.

Greece imports manufactured products of all kinds, because she is not an industrial country, and she imports fuel because she has no coal or oil of her own. Most of her imports come from Great Britain, the United States and Germany, to whom in turn she sends most of her exports.

A great many Greek men who work in industry work in the textile plants where they make both cotton and woollen materials. Most of the cotton and some of the wool for this most important of all Greek industries is grown in the country.

Many Greeks also work in chemical and food-processing industries. All of these are located around Athens and her port of

Piraeus, where there is a good supply of electric power and a good transport system.

Transport in Greece was completely disrupted during the war. Trucks, cars, buses and trains were lost and destroyed. Roads and bridges and railway lines were blown up. The difficult task of repairing these and restoring them to normal use is today complete. Buses and cars can now reach all the important towns on fairly good roads. In the mountains, however, donkey trails and goat paths are still more common than roads, and for a great number of people the donkey or the mule is still the most important means of transport.

There are railway lines which connect Greece directly with central Europe, but the lines connecting the various parts of the country are few. The routes the railway must follow go up and down, sometimes almost vertically, and zig-zag dizzily along the winding coast. This up-and-down, zig-zag business makes the building of a railway a very expensive business.

These transport difficulties, however, are made up for in part by the ease of sea travel. With many small but safe harbours all along the coast, it has always been a Greek habit to travel by sea. Small coasting steamers for passengers and cargo are familiar sights everywhere, even though air travel is becoming increasingly important. To reach all but three of the islands, for instance, it is possible to go only by sea.

CORINTH CANAL

ISLAND OF CRETE

The islands of Greece surround mainland Greece on all sides. Large islands, small islands, islands with pine woods and orchards and vineyards, and fields with men at work threshing grain or planting rice—islands which are no more than bits of rock encircled with white waves and hovered over by screeching seagulls and wild doves—hundreds of islands sparkling in the bright sea, all similar in some ways and yet each a distinct personality.

The best known of the islands in the Ionian Sea are Corfu, with

its Venetian castles and lovely beaches, and Ithaca, home of the wandering Ulysses. The peaceful charm of the Ionian islands has been destroyed many times by devastating earthquakes.

The largest of all Greek islands is Crete, a wild mountainous island in the Mediterranean—an island of ancient legends and priceless monuments, home of the famous painter El Greco. There are rich pastures on this island, forests, citrus and olive groves. Crete's history goes back 4,000 years.

The islands of the Aegean Sea are more numerous and more clustered than those of the Ionian. The Aegean itself, emerald and calm at times, has great outbursts of fury when huge waves, whipped by the wind, lash and tear at the islands.

Near the shores of Turkey lie the Dodecanese Islands, famous for Rhodes, the island of scholars and roses, and famous too for the bath sponges the islands produce for Britain and America. Many of the Greeks from the Dodecanese who emigrate to America settle at Tarpon Springs, Florida, where they carry on their traditional work of fishing for sponges.

The Cyclades, legendary islands with romantic names, lie in the middle of the Aegean. These islands were called the Cyclades in antiquity because they seemed to dance in a circle around Delos, the holy island, the birthplace of Apollo. Long ago the city of Delos was a religious, artistic and commercial centre. From all over Greece, worshippers came by the thousand, bringing sheep and cattle to be sacrificed to Apollo. But Apollo is dead now, and the island of Delos is deserted—strewn with broken columns and carvings and inscriptions and statues. The only people one sees now are the tourists.

It is difficult to say which of the many Aegean islands is the most delightful. Each has its own charm, but Skyros, near Delos, is particularly appealing. The town itself stands on a precipitous rock, and the town centre is reached by streets which are almost staircases. As you climb these narrow, winding streets, you can look into the main rooms of the houses. On white walls hang shining copper pans. There are bright cushions, carved wooden chairs and chests, and huge recessed open fireplaces. These delightful, white, wind-washed homes climb the rocks above the blue sea straight up into an even more brilliantly blue sky.

The houses and chapels of the Aegean islands are all a blinding white, as are the windmills scattered on the cliffs and hills above some of the towns. From the sea the harbour towns look like arrangements of little white cubes, curiously modern. In the moonlight they look bewitched.

The people of the islands do endless battle with the sea. Surrounded by it, threatened by its storms, living with it every day of their lives, the Greeks know well both the dangers and the gifts of the sea.

When island boys are very young, they begin their apprenticeship to the sea. Running barefoot on the rocks, they poke in the pools for shellfish. Soon they learn how to manage a tiny boat, how to fish, how to go octopus hunting. (It takes two to catch an octopus—one to paddle the boat and one to spear the fish, which is then beaten on a rock to make it tender for eating.) Fathers take their boys, when still very young, out to sea, and teach them how to navigate—where the rocks are, the names of the various islands, the safest harbours, the best spots for fish.

OCTOPUS HUNTING

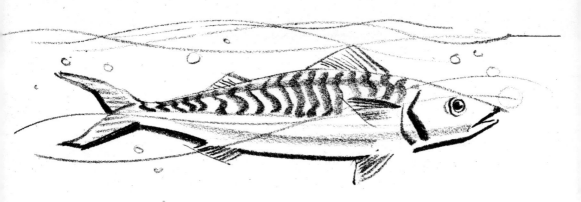

Fish, of course, is the main food in all fishing villages—all kinds of fish. Fried, boiled, grilled, or made into a delicious soup, it is eaten every day. In the evenings the little taverns on the islands are filled with the smell of fish frying and with the sounds of men laughing and singing and eating.

The songs they sing are swift and cheerful. They are usually accompanied by instruments—violin, zither, mandoline and lute. Sometimes the men dance. Greek music and dancing are best seen during the *panegyri*. This is the time when all the villages celebrate their patron saints with a festival and fair. Each village has its own saint, and each saint his church. On the evening of the saint's day, everyone dresses in his best clothes and goes to the decorated church. After the religious service the people make merry—dancing and singing all night, only to begin again the next evening in some other village for some other saint. In the season of panegyri many love affairs are started and many marriages arranged.

53

Fishing in the islands is done mostly with drag-nets. Where there is a beach, the net is hauled in to shore. Where there are only steep cliffs sliding into the sea, the net is hauled into a fishing boat. On some islands the fishermen go out to the open sea in motor vessels, while others use little motorboats near shore.

At evening the *gri-gri* boats go out. These are tiny boats, each with a big acetylene lamp. You can see them in the dark, their lamps sparkling and bobbing in the blackness, waiting through the night until the fish, attracted by the flame, swim into the nets. The catch of the gri-gri boats is collected by *caïques* and neatly packed in ice.

The caïques are almost an emblem of Greece. They are seen everywhere, sailing up and down the coasts, in and out of the harbours, inlets and bays. Their bright stripes of colour, their fine rigging and billowing sails bring an air of daring and adventure

PORT OF PIRAEUS

into the commerce of the sea. Loaded with fish, charcoal and gravel, food and provisions of all kinds, they tie up at the quays marked especially for them in the harbours.

The harbour of Piraeus, six miles from Athens, is the largest harbour in Greece. A fascinating place, like all harbours. Piraeus is a whirl of busy-ness — cargoes being loaded and unloaded, whistles hooting, men shouting; baskets, boxes, crates and even black goats being herded and hauled aboard or lowered ashore — coalers, tankers and tugs, sleek passenger ships from Europe and America.

55

small island steamers, tiny rowing boats, big ships and traders from all over the world, and always the caïques.

Piraeus, although the largest, is only one of many harbours from which the famous Greek fleets and merchant ships have always set sail. Since ancient times, Greeks have been seafarers—colonizers in the early days as well as traders, daring adventurers who went forth and took for Greece the great cities in Asia Minor, large areas in southern Italy and Sicily, part of the northern coast of Africa, a trading centre in Egypt, and settlements as far west as France and Spain. Greece, or Hellas as it was called in those days, was the supreme European Power until Rome succeeded in making it a Roman province in 146 B.C.

In spite of the Roman conquest, however, the genius of ancient Greece continued to influence the whole of western civilization for many hundreds of years. Greek thought, art and culture lived on and eventually created the civilization of western Europe.

Ideas such as liberty under the law, democracy, justice, free speech and free discussion had their beginnings in ancient Athens.

At that time these were new ideas in a world accustomed to being ruled by tyrants. But, in much later years, they became the ideals which greatly influenced the formation of our own parliament, and inspired men everywhere who believed in "life, liberty, and the pursuit of happiness".

In A.D. 395, when the Roman Empire was divided in half, the eastern provinces were formed into what was known as the Byzantine Empire. This empire was actually a blending of Roman, Greek and Oriental elements but by A.D. 600 Greek had replaced the Latin of the conquering Romans as the language of scholarship, government and the Church, as well as that of everyday life. The learning, art and philosophy of Greece influenced all the thinking, and the foundations of Christian teaching as we know it today were laid in the early years of this Byzantine period. And, as the Greek Church went forth and influenced neighbouring countries, so did this Byzantine, or mediaeval Greek, culture.

During the height of the Byzantine era, Constantinople, the capital of the empire, became the largest and wealthiest city of the Middle Ages. The palace of the emperor had banqueting halls with doors of silver and tables of gold, silver and rich enamel. Floors were strewn with roses and myrtle. Water tinkled in fountains set in lavish gardens, and in the stables costly race-horses snorted and tossed their manes.

This enormous wealth came from the empire's great industry

and commerce, for Constantinople was the crossroads of the east and west—a great trading centre and the home of a teeming industrial life.

In 1453 the Turks captured Constantinople and the Byzantine Empire fell. In 1821, almost 400 years later, the Greek struggle for liberation began. This War of Independence lasted until 1828, when an armistice was enforced. It was not until four years later, however, that Greece was finally recognized as an independent nation. The oppressive rule of the Turks was over and Greece, although faced by many difficulties, was again free.

GREEK WARRIOR

Down through the ages Greece has fought bravely many times for her liberty, and in World War II she set an example to the whole world of unprecedented bravery and devotion to her ancient ideals. Today Greece is a monarchy with a king and a queen at the head of the state. The king appoints a prime minister who, with his cabinet, is subject to the approval of and is responsible to the Parliament. Members of Parliament are elected by the people. In Greece the king reigns but he does not rule. The prime minister is actually the head of the government.

Greece is a member of the United Nations and of the North Atlantic Treaty Organization, and Greece today, as always, is democratic and passionately attached to freedom.

Freedom-loving and beauty-loving—this best describes the people of Greece. Despite its long and troubled history, Greece today is a young nation with a people enthusiastic and imaginative and full of hope for the future. "*Cherete!*" they call to one another. "Rejoice!"

"*Cherete!*" we call to Greece. "*Cherete,* friends!"

HISTORY

B.C.

circa 3000—Minoan and Mycenaean civilizations are born in Crete and the Peloponnesus.

circa 950—Homer's *Iliad*, the first great European literary work, narrates story of the siege of Troy.

750–500—Greeks establish cities in Asia Minor, Egypt, Italy, Sicily and France.

490—Athenians defeat the Persian invaders at Marathon.

477–431—The "Golden Age" of Greece. Drama, architecture and sculpture attain their highest expression, and ideals of democracy are formulated.

336–323—Alexander the Great overthrows Persian Empire and spreads Hellenic culture as far east as India.

146—Romans become masters of Greece.

A.D.

50—The Apostle Paul comes to Greece on first missionary venture in Europe. Greek is the language in which Christianity spreads in eastern Mediterranean.

330—Constantinople becomes capital of Christian Roman Empire.

circa 600—Byzantine Empire, long under the influence of Greek culture, is hellenized through peaceful evolution. This empire lasts until 1453.

1453—The Ottoman Turks take Constantinople, and Greece begins life under Turkish rule.

1821—Greek War of Independence begins.

1832—Greece becomes an independent kingdom.

1863—Britain cedes Ionian Islands to Greece.

1881—Turkey cedes Thessaly and part of Epirus to Greece.

1912–1913—Balkan Wars at end of which Greece receives Epirus, Macedonia, the Aegean Islands, Crete and part of Thrace.

1917—Greece enters war on side of the allies.

1919–1923—Greco–Turkish war.

1924—Greece is declared a republic.

1935—George II restored to throne.

1940—Italian invasion of Greece routed by Greek troops.

1941—Germany invades Greece and occupies country together with Italians and Bulgarians.

1944—Germans evacuate Greece. Greek government returns to Athens, faces communist rebellion.

1944–1949—Communist uprising and guerrilla warfare continues.

1947—Paul I becomes king. Italian Peace Treaty awards Dodecanese Islands to Greece.

1948–1949—Communist uprising put down.

1952—Greece admitted to NATO.

INDEX